Still Waiting

Still Waiting

Seeking God While Facing the Challenge of Infertility

E L I Z A B E T H   R O B E R T S O N

© 2011 by Elizabeth Robertson. All rights reserved.

WinePress Publishing (PO Box 428, Enumclaw, WA 98022) functions only as book publisher. As such, the ultimate design, content, editorial accuracy, and views expressed or implied in this work are those of the author.

No part of this publication may be reproduced, stored in a retrieval system, or transmitted in any way by any means—electronic, mechanical, photocopy, recording, or otherwise—without the prior permission of the copyright holder, except as provided by USA copyright law.

Unless otherwise noted, all Scriptures are taken from the *Holy Bible, New International Version®, NIV®*. Copyright © 1973, 1978, 1984 by Biblica, Inc.™ Used by permission of Zondervan. All rights reserved worldwide. www.zondervan.com

ISBN 13: 978-1-4141-1815-4
ISBN 10: 1-4141-1815-5
Library of Congress Catalog Card Number: 2010907388

Contents

Preface vii

Part I: Addressing the Issues

Chapter 1: Gaining Perspective 1
Chapter 2: The Struggle for Contentment 13
Chapter 3: Exploring Negative Emotions 21

Part II: Our Response

Chapter 4: Praise and Prayer 31
Chapter 5: Focus on Being a Godly Wife 41
Chapter 6: Time and Service 49

Additional Resources 57

Facilitator's Guide 59

Preface

INFERTILITY IS A difficult journey, a path that most people do not expect to take. My husband and I were surprised when we found ourselves traveling this road along with countless other couples. After more than a year of trying to conceive, we decided to seek help from a fertility specialist. We had no idea about all the testing and treatments involved in assisted reproductive technologies. I became pregnant right before taking a fertility medicine. About a year after our daughter was born, we decided to try for a second child. Once again, I was unable to become pregnant. We tried several drugs and fertility treatments, but after five years, we have not been able to have more children. Both my husband and I still yearn for another child, but we have accepted God's plan for us. We both believe that if it had been God's will for us to conceive again, one of the treatments would have resulted in a successful pregnancy.

God laid it on my heart to write a Bible study for couples dealing with infertility. For many, even within the church, infertility is a long, silent struggle. The need for support and understanding is very real, but resources are difficult to find. The purpose of this study is to provide a framework of discussion for important issues that might not be addressed in other venues. My hope is that readers will gain insight and encouragement through sharing experiences with each other and that they will develop a more godly, balanced perspective while pursuing the goals of parenthood. My aim is also to empower readers to use their time and talents wisely while waiting for God to fulfill their ultimate desire—a child. My prayer is that readers will always have faith to trust God, no matter what happens.

PART I
Addressing the Issues

CHAPTER 1

Gaining Perspective

WHEN DEALING WITH infertility, it is vitally important to remember the character and attributes of God. If we keep our minds focused on God, we will have the proper perspective in addressing any problem. When we experience difficult times in life, it is easy to lose sight of how powerful God truly is. Even though we may be aware of God's presence, our own feelings and anxious thoughts can distract from the unbelievable love and concern God extends to us every day, all the time.

GOD IS SOVEREIGN

Our God is the all-powerful ruler of the universe. He is perfect and holy, gracious and compassionate. He is the Creator of all things. Read the following verses that describe God and His character. Write down God's key attributes as described in each passage.

Psalm 74:12–17

_____

_____

Still Waiting

Psalm 89:6–8

Psalm 116:5

Psalm 145:8–19

Isaiah 40:26–31

Lamentations 3:22–23

What does it mean to you that God is compassionate?

When God does not grant us our requests, it is natural for us to ask why. However, we must recognize we cannot always comprehend the ways of God. He is everlasting and all-knowing. He is able to see the past, the present, and the future all at the same time. He is able

Gaining Perspective

to simultaneously see, hear, and care about every person in the world. Read the following verses about God's ways. Write down key ideas to encourage your heart in the days to come.

Psalm 18:30

_____

_____

Psalm 25:10

_____

_____

Psalm 33:11

_____

_____

Psalm 135:6–7

_____

_____

Ecclesiastes 11:5

_____

_____

Isaiah 55:8–9

_____

_____

Still Waiting

Romans 11:33–34

_____

_____

Think about all the painful things in life that are difficult to understand. Consider John the Baptist, whose parents consecrated him to God. He spent his entire life telling others the Good News and preparing the way for Jesus. Yet, he ended up suffering in prison. Do you think he ever wondered why? Don't you think he probably hoped that Jesus would have him set free, or at least that Jesus would have come to visit him? When John was beheaded, many of his followers were probably shocked that God allowed this to happen.

Why do you think God allows people to go through pain or suffering?

_____

_____

_____

Most of the time God's purpose and His plans are not obvious to us. We must continually trust in His infinite wisdom. Infertility is upsetting and emotionally exhausting, but we can choose to rely on our knowledge of God's loving kindness to strengthen our minds and hearts during this time. God's perfect will may seem confusing or unfair, and it is often not what we had in mind, but God wants only the best for us. He does not make mistakes. Psalm 145:17 tells us,

> *The Lord is righteous in all his ways and loving toward all he has made.*

GOD IS IN CONTROL

One of the most challenging aspects of dealing with infertility is our lack of control over our own bodies. We all like to have control in our lives, in our families, in our work, and in how we use our time.

Gaining Perspective

What are some examples of things that we do have control of in our lives?

_____

_____

_____

    It is difficult to realize that we have no ability to control what happens inside the uterus. Although we are involved in the reproductive process, we cannot affect the outcome. The result of our efforts is purely up to God. Only He can cause an egg to be fertilized, take root, and grow. Only God determines whether a pregnancy will be successful or not. Read the following verses about pregnancy. Again, write down key words to help you remember how God is our help when facing infertility.

Genesis 29:31

_____

_____

Genesis 30:22

_____

_____

1 Samuel 1:19–20

_____

_____

Job 39:1–3

_____

_____

Still Waiting

Psalm 139:13–16

God is in control of every detail, from conception to birth. God is able to overcome any obstacle if it is His will for us to have a child. God is not limited by our abilities. Medical factors are meaningless to Him. Matthew 19:26 reads:

Jesus looked at them and said, "With man this is impossible, but with God all things are possible."

One of the first couples we encounter in the Bible who struggled with infertility is Abraham and Sarah. In Genesis 12:2, God calls Abraham and promises him, "I will make you into a great nation and I will bless you." (Also read Genesis 15:1–6.) Abraham and Sarah did not have any children, so Abraham certainly must have wondered how God would make him into a nation. In Genesis 15:2–3, Abraham finally asks God directly, "What can you give me since I remain childless?" In verse four, God responds by promising him that he will indeed have an heir—a son from his own body. Despite having the assurance of God's promise, Abraham and Sarah dealt with infertility for many long years.

Do you think Sarah experienced any negative feelings or negative comments because of her inability to become pregnant? If so, how do you think she responded?

In Genesis 18:1–15, twenty-four years after God's promise, visitors come and tell Abraham that he and Sarah will have a child during the

Gaining Perspective

next year. Sarah overhears the news and laughs. Sarah was quite old and had probably passed menopause. How would you have reacted to this news?

_____

_____

_____

Throughout the Bible, Abraham was praised for his great faith in God. From a human perspective, it would have been easy for Abraham to doubt God's plan or God's timing. Read Romans 4:18–22, which reaffirms that Abraham steadfastly believed God would keep His promise.

GOD KNOWS US

God knows when we feel downhearted, angry, or stressed about not having children. He knows everything about us—all our fears and worries, all our faults and insecurities, all our efforts and failures. He deeply cares for us and understands our struggles. He knows all our thoughts. Read the following verses about God's knowledge and compassion. Write some notes to remind you of God's love and understanding.

Psalm 55:22

_____

_____

Psalm 68:19

_____

_____

Psalm 71:19–21

_____

_____

Still Waiting

Psalm 139:1–4

_____

_____

Matthew 6:25–27

_____

_____

Matthew 10:30

_____

_____

God knows infertility is difficult to deal with, but He promises to be with us and to help us. No matter what we face, we can depend on God. Read the following verses about God's strength. Write down some key words to help you remember how loving and protective God is.

Deuteronomy 31:6

_____

_____

Psalm 9:9–10

_____

_____

Psalm 29:11

_____

_____

Gaining Perspective

Psalm 32:8

_____

_____

Psalm 46:1

_____

_____

Psalm 62:5–8

_____

_____

Psalm 121

_____

_____

When do you most rely on God's strength?

_____

_____

GOD PROVIDES WHAT WE NEED

God knows exactly what each person needs, and He has promised always to provide our needs. He also knows our wants, plans, and dreams, but He doesn't promise to fulfill all of those wants, plans, and dreams. Sometimes what we want is in line with His will for us, but at other times our ideas are completely different from His. We should not expect God to conform His plan to ours so that our requests are met. He does not exist to satisfy our desires. Remember, He is in control of all things and has His own reasons for everything that happens. Deuteronomy 32:4 reads:

He is the Rock, his works are perfect, and all his ways are just. A faithful God who does no wrong, upright and just is he.

If we do not receive the child we hope for, we should remember that God promises to provide everything we *need*. He knows what we need better than we do because He made us. God is able to do anything, and He has infinite resources at His disposal. He does not withhold good things from us. We must trust that He knows what is ultimately best for us. Read the following verses about God's provision. Write down key thoughts for encouragement in days to come.

Psalm 23

_____

_____

Psalm 84:11

_____

_____

Isaiah 48:17

_____

_____

Romans 8:32

_____

_____

Gaining Perspective

Philippians 4:19

_____

_____

2 Peter 1:3

_____

_____

Besides meeting our daily physical needs, God promises to provide what we need emotionally and spiritually. He understands when we feel lonely or fearful, and when we have a need for intimacy or companionship. God's provision goes far beyond what we even ask. Read the following verses and write down reminders about all that God gives to us.

Psalm 73:23–26

_____

_____

Psalm 103:2–5

_____

_____

Ephesians 1:18–19

_____

_____

1 Peter 1:3–5

_____

_____

Still Waiting

God is not limited in any way. Remember Ephesians 3:20, which reads:

Now to him who is able to do immeasurably more than all we ask or imagine, according to his power that is at work within us.

Let your heart be joyful, knowing that God wants to bless you more than you can possibly imagine.

CHAPTER 2

The Struggle for Contentment

CONTENTMENT IS ONE of the main issues we must resolve when dealing with infertility. Being dissatisfied and wanting more is central to our unhappiness and impatience during this process. We need to look deeply at our attitudes and discover what is preventing us from appreciating and accepting all that God has given us.

Comparison with others

One of the reasons we often feel discontented with our situation is because we compare our lives to those of others. Although we may not intend to, there is an inevitable tendency to concentrate on what we do not have. That is precisely the challenge of obeying the tenth commandment, "You shall not covet...anything that belongs to your neighbor" (Ex. 20:17). Sometimes we feel great about our lives until we compare our circumstances to another's and see a disparity between the two. Instead of being thankful for our blessings, we become aware that something is lacking.

What, besides children, do you tend to notice that others have?

_____

_____

_____

Still Waiting

In the Bible, Jesus told the parable of the lost son (or the prodigal son) to describe how God responds when someone repents and chooses to have a relationship with Him. However, the reaction of the older brother is quite interesting. The servants come to tell him that the younger brother has finally returned and that they are having a big party to welcome him home. Luke 15:28 reads, "The older brother became angry and refused to go in." In Luke 15:29 he tells his father, "Look! All these years I've been slaving for you and never disobeyed your orders. Yet you never gave me even a young goat so I could celebrate with my friends."

Do you think the older brother was unhappy working for his father, or did he change his feelings when he saw how his father treated his younger brother?

_____

_____

_____

After hearing his complaint, the father tells the older brother that he had access to everything all those years. "'My son,' the father replied, 'you are always with me, and everything I have is yours'" (Luke 15:31). The older son's issue was not that he was deprived, but that he didn't realize or appreciate what he had. We, like the faithful son, have the privilege of knowing God and being able to approach Him anytime. We also have many, many blessings in our lives that God has provided for us, and continues to provide every day.

How do you think God feels when we are discouraged about our infertility?

_____

_____

_____

The Struggle for Contentment

IMPATIENCE

Another factor that may contribute to feelings of discontentment is impatience. In this culture of instant gratification, it is often difficult to wait even a week for something, much less for a month or more. Today we do not have to wait for stores to open; they are open twenty-four hours a day. We do not have to wait for an item to be in stock; we can buy it online. We do not have to save our money for an item. We can just buy the item with a credit card. Computers have facilitated our ability to gather information and goods from all over the world in a matter of seconds. When it comes to fertility, however, waiting is part of the process.

Many women use some sort of birth control earlier in their lives in order to prevent pregnancy, so it may come as a surprise when they do not immediately become pregnant after discontinuing their medication (or use of a contraceptive device). Age may also be a factor. Some women do not start trying to have children until their 30s and then expect everything to work according to their timeline. Try to keep in mind that just because something does not happen when we want it to, does not mean that it will not happen in the future. It may very well be part of God's plan for you to have children, but His idea of perfect timing may be very different from yours.

In the Bible, Abraham was one hundred years old, and Sarah was ninety years old when they finally had their son Isaac, (see Gen. 17:17; 21:5). Can you imagine waiting your entire life to become pregnant? Later, Isaac and Rebekah struggled to have children. They ended up waiting for twenty years to have their twins, Jacob and Esau (see Gen. 25:20, 26).

Did you expect to become pregnant right away?

_____

_____

_____

Still Waiting

Being patient for years is a constant battle. It is clear that when women in the Old Testament faced infertility, they did not always wait on God to change their situation. The Bible tells us in Genesis 16:1–5 that after ten years of not being able to conceive, Sarah decided to use her own method to solve the problem. She told Abraham, "The LORD has kept me from having children. Go, sleep with my maidservant; perhaps I can build a family through her" (Gen. 16:2). Later, in Genesis 30:3, Rachel chose to do the same thing: she offered her husband, Jacob, her maidservant in an effort to have children.

Today most women do not have servants, but even if they did, they would not offer them to their husbands as substitutes in order to have children. Do you think using current reproductive technologies is a way that couples today take matters into their own hands to accelerate the process? Why or why not?

_____

_____

_____

Having the patience to wait for good things in life can have a huge impact on our feelings of contentment with our day-to-day circumstances. Remember that each egg released into a woman's womb is unique. God may be waiting until a specific month when a particular egg is released to give you exactly the right child.

JEALOUSY

Another challenge for women dealing with infertility is to rejoice in a genuine way with those who are expecting or who already have children. There is a natural tendency to be jealous, not necessarily because of the actual children, but because of the experience of having children. However, when a woman feels jealous, she is often viewing motherhood in a very idealistic way. When a person sees a beautiful, precious baby, he or she is not thinking of midnight feedings, stinky diapers, spit up, crying, worry, and exhaustion. It is the love and bonding and the joy of seeing a child grow and develop that people wish for. The reality is that with the blessing of children come inconveniences as well. Jealousy wears rose-colored glasses.

Do you think you are realistic about the demands of motherhood? Why or why not?

_____

_____

_____

Women who have no trouble getting pregnant are sometimes insensitive to and completely unaware of the feelings of women who are struggling to conceive. When we have an unfulfilled desire for children, it can be difficult to acknowledge that God gives children to teenagers and single women who do not even want them. God does not give women children because they deserve them, or because they have earned them. We simply cannot always understand God's overall plan or His choices for each of us.

When seeing or interacting with a pregnant woman, what emotions have you experienced?

_____

_____

_____

In the Bible, women were sometimes competitive about having children. Rachel had the true love of her husband, but after seeing her sister, Leah, give birth to four sons, Rachel couldn't hold her emotions in any longer. Genesis 30:1 reads, "When Rachel saw that she was not bearing Jacob any children, she became jealous of her sister. So she said to Jacob, 'Give me children, or I'll die!'" Rachel was patient for probably about four years of her marriage, but when she finally did speak out, she seemed to blame her husband, rather than to admit her jealousy and her real desire to be equal with her sister.

Hannah also faced a similar problem with Peninnah, the other wife of her husband, Elkanah. The Bible tells us in 1 Samuel 1:6–7, "And because the LORD had closed her womb, her rival kept provoking her in order to irritate her. This went on year after year." The fact that Peninnah is recorded as Hannah's rival shows that there were tensions between the two women. Although we do not practice polygamy legally today, we may still experience the emotion of jealousy.

We cannot control what God gives us, but we *can* control our reactions. We should try to resist the temptation to be jealous of what others have that we do not. God knows what we can handle. He knows our strengths and weaknesses. He knows our desire to have children, and He also knows what is best for us. When we look at other people's lives, it is easy for us to feel that "their grass is greener than ours." We must realize that we are often not able to see the difficulties that other people face.

Spiritual Impediment

One reason we need to fight against discontentment is that it can adversely affect our witness as Christians in the world. Other people may not know that we are struggling with infertility but if our words and actions reveal feelings of disappointment or dissatisfaction with life, other people may certainly notice our displeasure. We do not have to be perpetually happy, but our lives should exude our ultimate trust in God and His will. Paul wrote in Philippians 4:11–13,

> *I have learned to be content whatever the circumstances. …I have learned the secret of being content in any and every situation, whether well fed or hungry, whether living in plenty or in want. I can do everything through him who gives me strength.*

We must rely on God's grace in order to be content and to fully accept God's plan for us.

The Struggle for Contentment

A second reason we need to fight against discontentment is that it can affect our own spiritual growth. Focusing on our own unfulfilled desires can hinder us from being all that God wants us to be and from doing all that God has designed for us to do. If we are continually bothered by the fact God has not granted our request for children, we are allowing this one area of our life to use time and energy that could be spent on other godly thoughts, activities, and ministries.

Jesus told a parable about a farmer who went out to sow his seed, and some of the seed "fell among thorns, which grew up and choked the plants, so they did not bear grain" (Mark 4:7). When Jesus explained the meaning of the parable, He said, "Others, like seed sown among thorns, hear the word; but the worries of this life, the deceitfulness of wealth and the desires for other things come in and choke the word, making it unfruitful" (Mark 4:18–19). Simply desiring that which we do not have can prevent us from producing fruit.

Can you think of anything that you could be doing for God or for the church that you have not been able to do because of dealing with infertility?

_____

_____

_____

In 2 Corinthians 12, Paul described his vision of heaven, and then in verses 7–9 wrote:

> To keep me from becoming conceited because of these surpassingly great revelations, there was given me a thorn in my flesh, a messenger of Satan, to torment me. Three times I pleaded with the Lord to take it away from me. But he said to me, "My grace is sufficient for you, for my power is made perfect in weakness."

In a sense, infertility is a thorn in our lives—a constant pain that we must bear every day, but God's grace is sufficient to help us with any problem

Still Waiting

we face. His power is made perfect in our weakness. God promises that the more we depend on Him, the more He will strengthen and sustain us.

Describe how God's grace has helped you through this time in your life.

_____

_____

_____

CHAPTER 3

Exploring Negative Emotions

MANY DIFFERENT EMOTIONS arise when dealing with infertility. We all have reactions to things that happen, but we often try to ignore them. We may not even realize the impact that infertility has had on our marriage. In this session, we will try to identify and analyze our feelings.

FRUSTRATION

There are many frustrations when dealing with infertility. Honestly, it takes great dedication to continually keep track of monthly cycles, days of ovulation, timing for intercourse, plus vitamins and medications. Perhaps the worst part is waiting the remaining weeks of the month only to once again menstruate. After many months of this vigilant process, it is natural to feel frustrated by a lack of results.

Sometimes there are physical problems in the female's body that may prevent pregnancy, such as endometriosis, fibroid tumors, poor egg quality, a previous illness, or other reproductive irregularities. There may also be problems with the male's body that may prevent pregnancy such as gland or hormone levels, low sperm count, illness, or other factors. Physical issues can be addressed by medical professionals. However, it is not as easy to treat the emotional impact caused by them.

Physical difficulties can often affect a person's self-esteem and can greatly diminish the enthusiasm with which he or she approaches the process of trying for a baby. Even if the spouse is very understanding, the other person will still be aware of the problem. It is important to remember that we really do not have control over our bodies. We are not at fault for any physical attribute that has become an obstacle for pregnancy. We are all created by God, and God does not make mistakes.

How has infertility affected your view of yourself and/or your husband?

_____

_____

_____

Frustration may occur if one spouse is more committed to the idea of having children than the other. The spouse who is less motivated may go along with the plans, but his or her attitude or demeanor may reveal true feelings. A spouse's lack of interest or lack of emotional involvement can be discouraging to the person who truly wants to continue trying for a child. Unfortunately, perception is sometimes the culprit. If a spouse is indeed committed to the process, but does not communicate it properly, the other spouse may not feel supported.

Do you ever sense that your husband does not feel as strongly as you do, or feels less urgency about the situation? Explain.

_____

_____

_____

For those trying to conceive by natural means, planned times for intimacy can be a challenge. It's great when sex is fun and passionate and spontaneous. It is not always the same when you *have* to do it. Between work responsibilities, busy schedules, travel, tiredness, or other factors, it can be difficult for either spouse to be in the right frame of mind when it is time to try for a baby. The stress and awareness of fertility

Exploring Negative Emotions

treatments (or physical discomfort) can also diminish romantic feelings. Even when both partners are willing and determined to make things work, the process may be less than ideal.

How have you kept the spark in your marriage?

_____

_____

_____

Another aspect of infertility that can be frustrating is not knowing whether pregnancy will occur. For those who enjoy planning ahead, it is very difficult to consider each month what would happen if a pregnancy were successful—when the baby would be born, taking time off work, child care issues, etc. Although this is not necessary, it is a natural inclination for goal-oriented people. Having to think about these different scenarios for the last two weeks of every cycle can be stressful and tiring. In addition, doctors recommend being careful about doing anything that may possibly harm the baby during the last two weeks of every cycle. Having to avoid medications such as pain relievers or antibiotics, caffeine, alcohol, aspartame, sushi, etc. every month can become wearisome. For those who try fertility treatments, having to adjust your schedule to fit in last-minute doctor appointments can also be a bother.

What is the most frustrating aspect of infertility for you?

_____

_____

_____

Sorrow

When we are not able to have the children that we so much want, it is normal for us to feel sadness about this unfulfilled desire. Sometimes it is difficult to deal with our feelings of disappointment without letting them hinder our joy in daily life. God knows our hearts and sees our longings, but He does not always choose to do what we ask. He does, however, promise to comfort us. In 2 Corinthians 1:3–4, Paul writes:

Praise be to the God and Father of our Lord Jesus Christ, the Father of compassion and the God of all comfort, who comforts us in all our troubles, so that we can comfort those in any trouble with the comfort we ourselves have received from God.

In the Bible, Hannah was a woman who was truly miserable about not being able to have children. After dealing with infertility for many years, her sorrow became overwhelming (see 1 Sam. 1:1–20). Her husband, Elkanah, loved her but was not able to understand her feelings. He said to her, "Hannah, why are you weeping? Why don't you eat? Why are you downhearted? Don't I mean more to you than ten sons?" When she went to the Temple, the Bible tells us, "In bitterness of soul Hannah wept much and prayed to the LORD" (1 Sam. 1:10). After being rebuked by Eli the priest because she appeared to be intoxicated, Hannah told him, "'I am a woman who is deeply troubled.... I have been praying here out of my great anguish and grief'" (1 Sam. 1:15–16).

How has God helped you deal with disappointment?

_____

_____

_____

Many women experience additional sorrow because of the loss of a child either through miscarriage, ectopic pregnancy, or through some other cause. This can be extremely painful especially when a successful pregnancy does not follow. Even in the darkest times God is merciful and loving. Psalm 34:18 tells us, "The LORD is close to the brokenhearted and saves those who are crushed in spirit." We cannot fully understand why God allows these things, but it is possible that He may have spared us and those children from great trials such as serious disabilities, illness, or early death. Read Isaiah 41:10 and Isaiah 43:1–2, and remember that God is always faithful.

RIDICULE AND EXPECTATIONS

Most of the time women who have had no difficulty conceiving have trouble understanding the challenge of infertility. It is a unique experience to deal with months (or years) of worry and disappointment, as well as decisions regarding fertility treatments. When interactions occur between a woman who is struggling with infertility and a woman who has two or more children, sometimes a certain insensitivity or subtle rejection may be felt by the infertile woman from the woman who is the mother of children. It may be a facial expression, a comment or question, or it may be from an obvious lack of attention or respect. It may simply be imagined because of the childless woman's insecurity. However, it is still worth addressing this relational issue. Sometimes even men in the church unintentionally assign more worth to mothers than to women without children.

In Bible times, women were expected to have children and were looked down upon if they failed to do so. In the Old Testament, Rachel definitely felt this kind of societal disapproval. Genesis 30:22–23 reads: "Then God remembered Rachel; he listened to her and opened her womb. She became pregnant and gave birth to a son and said, 'God has taken away my disgrace.'" Hannah also experienced derision, particularly from her husband's other wife. The scripture reads in 1 Samuel 1:6–7:

> And because the LORD had closed her womb, her rival kept provoking her in order to irritate her. This went on year after year. Whenever Hannah went up to the house of the LORD, her rival provoked her till she wept and would not eat.

In the New Testament, we find that Elizabeth, who was barren for many years, also dealt with derision. When she finally became pregnant, she said, "The Lord has done this for me.... In these days he has shown his favor and taken away my disgrace among the people" (Luke 1:25).

Still Waiting

Have you ever felt any kind of rejection or felt less important because you did not have children (or only had one child)? Explain.

_____

_____

_____

Besides dealing with our own and our spouse's desire for children, we must deal with other people's expectations as well. Because this influence is usually quite subtle, we may not even be aware of how it may erode our self-confidence or prevent us from feeling completely satisfied. Sometimes parents will verbally express their desire for grandchildren or will show their approval of friends or siblings who have children. Sometimes we have a group of friends with children, and we may feel motivated by their enthusiasm.

Have you ever felt pressured by other people to have a child (or more children)? Explain.

_____

_____

_____

Today, many couples decide not to have any children or to have only one. This choice is not always obvious to others, so often people will ask about family plans. Most people do not have any idea that we are dealing with infertility unless we have talked about it with them. Usually, friends are just curious and do not intend to hurt our feelings or infer anything about our lack of numerous children. However, even if we are at peace about our situation, these personal questions can be disconcerting and can unravel our emotional state.

Exploring Negative Emotions

Have you ever felt uncomfortable when someone has asked about your plans to have children (or more children)? Explain.

_____

_____

_____

MOTIVES

Sometimes women decide they would like to have a child in order to improve their relationship with a spouse. Unfortunately, this is not a good motive for having children. Both pregnancy and raising a child create major sources of stress. Having a baby typically does not help to solidify an already strained relationship. If there are issues with communication, finances, parents, dependencies, or other areas, couples should address those issues, either within the marriage or through a counselor. Spouses may also have very different views regarding how to teach and discipline children, so it is a good idea for couples to discuss proposed parenting techniques and opinions before a child is born.

In the Bible, Leah was married to a man who did not love her. Genesis 29:31 reads, "When the LORD saw that Leah was not loved, he opened her womb." God knew what Leah needed and gave her children to comfort her. However, Leah's motivation for having children was to gain the love of her spouse. After giving birth to her first son, she said, "Surely my husband will love me now." (Gen. 29:32). After having her third son, she said, "Now at last my husband will become attached to me, because I have borne him three sons" (Gen. 29:34). Years later, after she bore her sixth son, she said, "God has presented me with a precious gift. This time my husband will treat me with honor, because I have borne him six sons" (Gen. 30:20). Unfortunately, Leah never really did gain the love of Jacob, but she was dearly loved by God.

Still Waiting

Have you ever known someone who had misdirected motives for getting pregnant other than just wanting children? If so, how did you feel about it? What was the outcome?

_____

_____

_____

The desire to have children is completely natural. God commanded us to be fruitful and multiply. But we should not want children for reasons other than to serve Him and to glorify Him by raising up godly children. Remember that the most important thing in life is your relationship with God, not reproduction. Read Psalm 51:10–12, and pray that God will purify your heart and help you always put Him first in your life.

PART II
Our Response

CHAPTER 4

Praise and Prayer

IN THIS CHAPTER, we will focus on what our spiritual response should be when dealing with the challenge of infertility. No matter what difficulty we face we need to be thankful and to seek God and His will for us.

Praise God consistently

We were created to glorify God. The most important thing we can do is to love the Lord and worship Him. Our praise should not be dependent upon whether or not God gives us the children we desire. We are to praise God at all times no matter how we feel and no matter what our situation. God deserves our continuous worship, adoration, and thanksgiving for who He is, for all He has done, and for all that He will do in the future. Read the following verses and write down key ideas about gratefulness.

Psalm 100:4–5

_____

_____

Still Waiting

Colossians 2:6–7

_____

_____

1 Thessalonians 5:18

_____

_____

Hebrews 13:15

_____

_____

Fixing our eyes on Christ takes our focus off ourselves and our desires. David is an excellent example of someone in the Bible who endured many trials. Yet even in his darkest hours, he was steadfast in his worship of and devotion to God. In Psalm 42:5–6 David wrote, "Why are you downcast, O my soul? Why so disturbed within me? Put your hope in God, for I will yet praise him, my Savior and my God." Read Psalm 86:1–12 and Psalm 145.

How does worshiping God help you through difficult times?

_____

_____

_____

There are many different ways to glorify God. We can thank God for all His attributes. We can tell other people about God and all that He has done, both throughout history and in our own lives. When we talk about our faith or share our testimony, we are honoring God.

Praise and Prayer

We can also sing to God. Psalm 95:1–2 reads, "Come, let us sing for joy to the LORD; let us shout aloud to the Rock of our salvation. Let us come before him with thanksgiving and extol him with music and song." Psalm 105:2 reads, "Sing to him, sing praise to him; tell of all his wonderful acts."

Another way we can glorify God is by the way we live. In Romans 12:1 Paul writes, "Therefore, I urge you, brothers, in view of God's mercy, to offer your bodies as living sacrifices, holy and pleasing to God—this is your spiritual act of worship." When we do our best to obey God's commands and to live a holy life, we show God that we love Him. When we work to pursue excellence, to serve others, or to demonstrate godly leadership, we are using our lives to praise God.

What are some other ways we can glorify God?

_____

_____

_____

It is difficult to truly worship God with all of your heart if you do not fully believe He will provide what you need. John 3:27 records, "To this John replied, 'A man can receive only what is given him from heaven.'" We need to be content with our place in life and the role God has asked us to fulfill. Our dreams may be for something else or something more, and God understands that.

In the Old Testament, after years and years of waiting, Rachel gave birth to her first son. In Genesis 30:24, the Bible records that her first response was to ask for more. "She named him Joseph, and said, 'May the LORD add to me another son.'" Unfortunately, when Rachel later had her second son, she passed away immediately after giving birth (see Gen. 35:16–18). We do not know what God has planned for us or why He may not have granted our request, but we must praise Him because He is the ruler of the universe, regardless of our own agenda.

Do you think it is human nature or the influences of society that cause us always to want more?

___

WAIT FOR THE LORD

The Bible tells us in Ecclesiastes 3:1–8 that there is a proper time for everything. We may think that now is a good time to have children, but that may not be God's plan for us. We must be patient and learn to wait on God's timing. Our view of the world is based on our limited perspective. God has unlimited knowledge of all people and all events. We are reminded of this in 2 Peter 3:8, "But do not forget this one thing, dear friends: With the Lord a day is like a thousand years, and a thousand years, are like a day." God's power is not confined by time.

How do you feel about God's timing?

___

Everyone makes plans at some point, but it is God who decides the ultimate outcome. We may try all sorts of things in an attempt to conceive or adopt, but it is God who determines whether we will have children. Proverbs 16:9 tells us, "In his heart a man plans his course, but the LORD determines his steps." It is good for us to be prepared and to have long-term goals, but we should acknowledge God in every area of our lives. Read Proverbs 16:1–3 and Psalm 20:4–5.

Is making plans ever wrong? Why or why not?

___

Praise and Prayer

In the Bible, David was a great example of someone who waited for the Lord to act in his behalf. David was anointed as the next king when he was very young (see 1 Sam. 16:13). He had to wait many years to actually become king. David's writings encourage us to trust that God has a plan. Read the following verses and note what they tell us about patience.

Psalm 27:14

_____

_____

Psalm 37:7

_____

_____

Psalm 130:5–6:

_____

_____

What does "waiting on the Lord" mean to you?

_____

_____

_____

God understands that people have needs, longings, and problems that cannot be easily solved. He also knows that dealing with these things can be mentally and physically exhausting. In Matthew 11:28–30, Jesus said,

> "Come to me, all you who are weary and burdened, and I will give you rest. Take my yoke upon you and learn from me, for I am gentle

and humble in heart, and you will find rest for your souls. For my yoke is easy and my burden is light."

To experience freedom and peace, we must surrender our desires and lay them at the feet of Jesus.

Why is it so difficult to surrender the desire for children?

_____

_____

_____

Seek God's will

Most importantly, we need to seek God's will first and foremost. In Matthew 6:9–10 Jesus taught, "This, then, is how you should pray: 'Our Father in heaven, hallowed be your name, your kingdom come, your will be done on earth as it is in heaven.'" Most of the time, we do not know exactly what God's will is, but if we pray and earnestly seek Him with a pure heart, God can work through us and can help us see things through His eyes. Romans 12:2 reads, "Do not conform any longer to the pattern of this world, but be transformed by the renewing of your mind. Then you will be able to test and approve what God's will is—his good, pleasing and perfect will."

How do you decide if something is God's will?

_____

_____

_____

If we do our best to make God's priorities our priorities, we may begin to perceive His will more clearly in our lives. We shouldn't constantly be worrying about whether or not we will have children; we should be focusing on our relationship with God and on telling

Praise and Prayer

others about His love. Jesus said in Matthew 6:33, "But seek first his kingdom and his righteousness, and all these things will be given to you as well." If we pursue the goals of sharing the gospel and living a holy life, God will provide what we need. Psalm 37:4 reads, "Delight yourself in the LORD and he will give you the desires of your heart."

What are some ways we can delight ourselves in the Lord?

_____

_____

_____

CONTINUE TO PRAY

We may feel that when we pray, we ask too much or too often, but the truth is that God wants us to pray, and He listens to us. He does not get tired of hearing our prayers and requests. Jesus taught that when we pray, we must have faith that God will grant our requests. Read the following verses and write down key ideas about prayer.

Matthew 21:21–22

_____

_____

Ephesians 3:12

_____

_____

Hebrews 4:16

_____

_____

Still Waiting

Romans 8:26–27

_____

_____

James 1:5–7

_____

_____

Why is it sometimes hard to maintain our belief that God will ultimately grant our request?

_____

_____

_____

In Luke 18:1–8, Jesus told a parable about a persistent widow who repeatedly asked an unjust judge to help her. The judge finally grew tired of her bothering him and granted her request. To explain this illustration, Jesus said, "And will not God bring about justice for his chosen ones, who cry out to him day and night? Will he keep putting them off? I tell you, he will see that they get justice, and quickly" (Luke 18:7–8). Unlike this unjust judge, God does not get irritated by our persistent prayers. First John 5:14–15 tells us,

> *This is the confidence we have in approaching God: that if we ask anything according to his will, he hears us. And if we know that he hears us—whatever we ask—we know that we have what we asked of him.*

Besides continuing to pray ourselves, we should also ask our spouse to pray with us and for us. The Bible tells us in Genesis 25:21, "Isaac prayed to the LORD on behalf of his wife, because she was barren. The

Praise and Prayer

LORD answered his prayer, and his wife Rebekah became pregnant." Keep in mind, however, that Isaac and Rebekah were married for twenty years before they had children, so Isaac may have been praying for a long time! Jesus said in Matthew 18:19–20, "Again, I tell you that if two of you on earth agree about anything you ask for, it will be done for you by my Father in heaven. For where two or three come together in my name, there am I with them."

Is it ever a challenge for you to ask someone to pray for you about your fertility? Explain why.

_____

_____

_____

Jesus taught us in Matthew 7:7–11:

"Ask and it will be given to you; seek and you will find; knock and the door will be opened to you. For everyone who asks receives; he who seeks finds; and to him who knocks, the door will be opened. Which of you, if his son asks for bread, will give him a stone? Or if he asks for a fish, will give him a snake? If you, then, though you are evil, know how to give good gifts to your children, how much more will your Father in heaven give good gifts to those who ask him!"

The words *knock, seek,* and *ask* all imply action. What type of actions do you think are appropriate when dealing with infertility?

_____

_____

_____

When we have to wait for many months or years for God's answer, we often become discouraged and sometimes pray less often (or quit praying) for that particular situation. Paul tells us in Romans 12:12, "Be joyful in hope, patient in affliction, faithful in prayer." He also wrote in Philippians 4:6–7:

> *Do not be anxious about anything, but in everything, by prayer and petition, with thanksgiving, present your requests to God. And the peace of God, which transcends all understanding, will guard your hearts and your minds in Christ Jesus.*

Resolve to pray every day, and have faith that God will answer your prayers.

CHAPTER 5

Focus on Being a Godly Wife

AS WE WAIT for God to reveal His will to us, our goal should be to develop into the person God intended us to be. Besides spending time with God and His word, we continually need to work towards being an excellent godly wife. If we do not have any children, then our main focus at home should be on our husband and our life with him. If we do have children (or other relatives living with us), then we must balance our efforts to take care of all our family members. One of the passages of the Bible that vividly describes an exemplary wife is Proverbs 31:10–31. Begin by reading these verses. In this chapter, we will look closely at some characteristics demonstrated by this woman.

TAKE CARE OF YOUR HUSBAND

Our primary duty as a godly wife is to bless our husband. Proverbs 31:12 reads, "She brings him good, not harm, all the days of her life." The word *brings* is an active verb. She does things to impact his life in a positive way. This responsibility and privilege involves serving our husband in many different ways. Proverbs 31:11 reads, "Her husband has full confidence in her and lacks nothing of value." A godly wife should be honest and faithful. She should use good judgment and be completely trustworthy.

One thing the godly wife does is she "provides food for her family" (Prov. 31:14–15). Although some men enjoy cooking and do so often, many men appreciate their wives taking responsibility for the purchase of groceries and meal preparation. If we truly desire to take care of our husbands, we should be aware of the nutritional content of what we provide for them to eat. We may also need to help our husbands watch what they eat and avoid excesses in sodium, trans-fats, cholesterol, and carbohydrates. In addition, our husband's diet may have other special requirements.

Do you find the responsibility of providing food to be a pleasure or a chore?

_____

_____

_____

    A godly wife also makes sure that her family is well clothed. Proverbs 31:21 reads, "When it snows, she has no fear for her household; for all of them are clothed in scarlet." The word *scarlet* indicates the highest quality. Many men today enjoy shopping for their own clothes to maintain their own distinct style. However, a wife can always help her husband with this aspect of life by knowing his preferences and their budget, and by looking for clothes that would fit his needs. Proverbs 31:21 also shows that the godly wife plans ahead for seasonal changes. She makes sure her husband has appropriate apparel for all kinds of weather.

    There are other aspects that could be considered part of making sure your husband is "well clothed." For example, sometimes he may need to make improvements in personal hygiene or personal grooming. Sometimes he may need to purge items from his wardrobe. At some point his hair style or his glasses may need to be updated. Proverbs 31:23 reads, "Her husband is respected at the city gate." If we desire respect by others for our husband, we should assist him in making sure his appearance is clean and presentable.

Focus on Being a Godly Wife

What do you do to help your husband be respected?

_____

_____

_____

Proverbs 31:22 tells us that the godly wife also, "makes coverings for her bed." Today most women choose to purchase a quilt or comforter and blankets and sheets rather than to make them by hand. However, the act of taking the initiative to go to the store and buy or order bedding can certainly be helpful to a busy husband. Providing other necessary household items, such as towels and dishes, would probably fit into this category. Decorating your home in a pleasing way is another thing that a wife can do to bless her husband.

In addition, Proverbs 31:27 tells us the godly wife "watches over the affairs of her household." She not only provides for the immediate needs of her husband, she also notices changes and looks ahead to future. She reflects on ideas and suggests things that may be beneficial. She may remind him of appointments, schedule dates together, or arrange for vacation plans. To take care of her husband more deeply, a godly wife must look to his emotional needs as well. He may need time to be alone. He may need time to relax or he may need a night out to have fun. He may need fellowship with other Christians or time to serve at church.

Perhaps most importantly, a godly wife should build up her husband as a person. She should make him feel accepted, appreciated, loved, and respected. Personal affirmations will make a huge difference in his life, and consequently, will greatly enhance your marriage relationship.

Do you ever have difficulty knowing what your husband needs? Explain.

_____

_____

_____

TAKE CARE OF YOURSELF

One duty we have as wives is to take care of our bodies. Proverbs 31:17 reads, "She sets about her work vigorously; her arms are strong for her tasks." We should not let ourselves become so out of shape that we do not have the ability to fulfill our responsibilities as wives. Exercise and good nutrition are important in order to have strength. In addition, exercise and eating well will prevent other health problems that may cause harm to our bodies. This is often a challenge, especially with the added stress of infertility.

Has dealing with infertility affected your desire to exercise? Explain.

_____

_____

_____

Taking care of ourselves includes looking after our appearance. Proverbs 31:22 reads, "She is clothed in fine linen and purple." In the Bible, linen was associated with nobility, and the color purple was linked with kings. Thus, we can assume that the godly wife of this passage was clothed beautifully. Our appearance is important, not only because we should be pleasing to our husband, but because to others, our appearance reflects on our husband.

Regarding our appearance, Paul wrote in 1 Timothy 2:9–10, "I also want women to dress modestly, with decency and propriety, not with braided hair or gold or pearls or expensive clothes, but with good deeds, appropriate for women who profess to worship God." Proverbs 31:30 reads, "Charm is deceptive, and beauty is fleeting; but a woman who fears the LORD is to be praised." The ideal wife is not described as gorgeous, glamorous, sexy, thin, or stylish. It is her faith and her relationship to God that are most important.

Focus on Being a Godly Wife

FULFILL RESPONSIBILITIES

It is clear that the godly wife of Proverbs 31 had servants to help her with household responsibilities, but she herself does many of the things women were expected to do. Proverbs 31:13 reads, "She selects wool and flax and works with eager hands," and Proverbs 31:19 reads, "In her hand she holds the distaff and grasps the spindle with her fingers." She takes the wool and flax and spins them into yarn, eventually making cloth. Proverbs 31:14–15 indicates that she provides food for her household, and verse 22 reads, "She makes coverings for her bed." Today women are not necessarily expected to make things by hand, such as clothes or bedding, but we are usually expected to help with everyday household duties such as doing dishes, cleaning and organizing the house, buying groceries, cooking, taking care of animals, taking out the trash, etc.

If you are worried or upset about infertility issues, do household responsibilities seem therapeutic or burdensome?

_____

_____

_____

FIND GOOD THINGS

One of the things that the exemplary wife does is to search for and purchase high quality items. Proverbs 31:13–14 reads: "She selects wool and flax and works with eager hands. She is like the merchant ships, bringing her food from afar." In other words, the wife of Proverbs 31 is a good shopper! She doesn't just buy wool and flax; she looks at what is available and chooses carefully. She doesn't just buy food; she finds items from far away for her husband to enjoy. Today we have many resources besides our local grocery stores and department stores. Whether we are searching for the best quality or the best value, we can help our husband by using money wisely and taking the time to provide him with a variety of good things from around the world.

Where do you enjoy searching for bargains or treasures?

_____

_____

_____

BE ENTERPRISING

The godly wife of Proverbs 31 is quite a skilled business woman. She is intelligent and independent and able to make decisions and investments on her own. Proverbs 31:16 reads, "She considers a field and buys it; out of her earnings she plants a vineyard." Not only does she purchase a piece of land, she uses her own money to turn it into a vineyard. Proverbs 31:18 reads, "She sees that her trading is profitable," and Proverbs 31:24 reads, "She makes linen garments and sells them, and supplies the merchants with sashes." It is not really clear as to whether this woman works inside her home or outside the home, and the passage does not reveal her exact motivation for working, but she obviously sells and trades and earns some sort of income.

Has infertility changed your attitude regarding having a career? How?

_____

_____

_____

BE COMPASSIONATE

The godly wife honors God by helping those in need. Proverbs 31:20 reads, "She opens her arms to the poor and extends her hands to the needy." She is kind and giving and generous. She also shares her knowledge with others and is able to give godly advice. Proverbs 31:26 tells us, "She speaks with wisdom, and faithful instruction is on her tongue." This woman seems incredibly busy, yet she is available and willing to take time to be a good friend and neighbor.

Focus on Being a Godly Wife

Has your struggle with infertility made you less able or more hesitant to assist others with their problems? Explain.

_____

_____

_____

BE INDUSTRIOUS

The godly wife definitely works hard. Proverbs 31:13 tells us that she, "works with eager hands." Verse 17 reads, "She sets about her work vigorously." Verse 27 reads that she "does not eat the bread of idleness." In addition, verse 15 reads, "She gets up while it is still dark," and verse 18 reads, "her lamp does not go out at night." In other words, the ideal woman of Proverbs 31 gets up early and stays up late in order to work for her family. Honestly, there is no way anyone could do all of the things listed in the previous sections without expending a great deal of effort. It is clear that the godly wife is not just busy with her own hobbies and interests but is always working to serve others and provide well for her household.

In our busy lives today, we often get up early and/or stay up late, but not always for the purpose of working. Even though we may intend to do more useful things with our time, we may end up watching TV, surfing the Internet, talking on the phone, or doing other recreational activities. If we are trying to cope with an emotional issue, anxiety and stress can actually use up our energy and hinder us from sleeping soundly.

When has dealing with infertility made it difficult for you to feel highly motivated?

_____

_____

_____

Still Waiting

Whether it is inside the house or outside the house, working hard each day can help maintain and improve your marriage. Being industrious and completing tasks gives a person a sense of purpose and accomplishment; it may help you to have a more positive attitude and to be less focused on the outcome of your fertility efforts. Working can also enhance your relationship with your husband because working provides you with experiences to share. First Corinthians 15:58 reads:

Therefore, my dear brothers, stand firm. Let nothing move you. Always give yourselves fully to the work of the Lord, because you know that your labor in the Lord is not in vain.

Remember that God knows your heart and sees all your efforts.

CHAPTER 6

Time and Service

IN THIS LAST chapter, we will discuss many ways we can use our time and find deeper fulfillment. One aspect of life that definitely changes with the addition of children is the amount of free time available. Therefore, while we are waiting for God to show us His will, we should appreciate the time that we have and use it wisely.

SERVE GOD

We should not live our lives only to please ourselves or someone else, nor should we resent the role and responsibilities God has given us. It doesn't matter how menial or how important our work may be. Ultimately, we are serving God. Paul wrote in Ephesians 6:7, "Serve wholeheartedly, as if you were serving the Lord, not men." We need to do everything with pure motives and with our maximum effort because we are working for the Lord, the Maker of heaven and earth. If indeed we are working for the one, true, holy, righteous, perfect, eternal God, we should care about the quality of our work. We should pursue excellence in all things.

Still Waiting

Do you feel that you are fully devoted to the tasks God has given you? Explain.

_____

_____

_____

Because we are not in control of our fertility, it is sometimes easy to forget that God *is* in control of it. We may feel that for some reason God is not allowing us to have children, but the truth is, God has something else for us to do—at least for now. Ephesians 2:10 reads,

For we are God's workmanship, created in Christ Jesus to do good works, which God prepared in advance for us to do.

God knows our personality and our abilities. He leads us to things that will benefit by our unique involvement. He brings us into contact with specific people whose lives will be enriched by our friendship. In addition, He provides for us so that we can do all He gives us to do. In 2 Corinthians 9:8 we read, "And God is able to make all grace abound to you, so that in all things at all times, having all that you need, you will abound in every good work." God provides all that we need and helps us with everything we do. Philippians 2:13 reads, "For it is God who works in you to will and to act according to his good purpose."

What other things may God have for you to do?

_____

_____

_____

USE YOUR TALENTS

God gives everyone certain strengths and abilities. Some people may be able to lead and organize events. Others would rather work in the

Time and Service

background. Some people may sing well or be able to play an instrument. Others are wonderful cooks or have the ability to sew clothing. Some people are excellent gardeners. Others are good at crafts or have an eye for decorating or scrapbooking. Some people excel at sports, while others like to read or spend time hiking or fishing. God gives us these abilities, but it is up to us to develop our potential and to use our talents. Sometimes we become so focused on having a child that we begin to feel less satisfied with our sense of identity and our contribution to the community.

What are some things that you are truly good at and that you enjoy?

_____

_____

_____

In the Old Testament, Deborah played an important part in the history of Israel. Although she was married, the Bible does not mention her having any children. Judges 4:4–5 reads: "Deborah, a prophetess, the wife of Lappidoth, was leading Israel at that time. She held court under the Palm of Deborah …and the Israelites came to her to have their disputes decided." Deborah worked as a judge for God's people. Judges 4:2–3 tells us that God allowed Jabin, the king of Canaan, to have control over Israel, and that Sisera, the commander of his army, cruelly oppressed the Israelites for twenty years. God chose Deborah to help the Israelite leader, Barak, defeat Sisera's army. When Deborah instructed Barak to go to battle, "Barak said to her, 'If you go with me, I will go; but if you don't go with me, I won't go.'" The Israelite commander evidently had great respect for Deborah, who was probably a very strong, intelligent leader. God helped Deborah to guide Barak and accomplish an important military victory.

In the New Testament, Priscilla and her husband, Aquila, were good friends of Paul the apostle (see Acts 18). Again, the Bible never mentions this couple having any children. When Paul left Corinth, he took Priscilla and Aquila with him to Ephesus, where he left them while he went on to Caesarea and Antioch. Priscilla and Aquila had a deep understanding of the gospel message. Acts 18: 24–28 tells us that Priscilla and Aquila befriended the evangelist Apollos, who "was a learned man, with a thorough knowledge of the Scriptures." God helped Priscilla and Aquila discern what was missing in Apollos's teaching, and they "explained to him the way of God more adequately." God used Priscilla and Aquila's intellectual and teaching abilities to provide greater insight for Apollos. It is interesting to note that even in a very male-dominated society, Priscilla's name is always listed first when the Bible mentions this couple.

God may have an important task or role that He wants us to fulfill, but if we are too busy to hear His voice, we may miss the opportunity. Although being a mother is a wonderful experience and may be our ultimate goal, God may have a completely different plan for us. We need to set aside our own wants and expectations and earnestly search for what God has for us to do. In 1 John 2:17 we read, "The world and its desires pass away, but the man who does the will of God lives forever."

Do you believe that you may be used by God to do something incredibly important?

_____

_____

_____

USE YOUR SPIRITUAL GIFTS

If you have accepted Jesus as your Lord and Savior, you have been given at least one, if not several, spiritual gifts through the Holy Spirit. Regarding spiritual gifts, 1 Corinthians 12:11 reads, "All these are the work of one and the same Spirit, and he gives them to each one, just as he determines." If you do not know what your spiritual gifts are, then it would be a good idea to complete some sort of gift assessment or to take a class to discover your spiritual gifts. In 1 Corinthians 12:7–10 and Ephesians 4:11–13, several of the spiritual gifts are specifically listed. Spiritual gifts may or may not correspond to your natural abilities.

Time and Service

Each Christian's gifts are meant to be used within the church to bless other believers and to benefit the Church as a whole. The Bible says in 1 Peter 4:10, "Each one should use whatever gift he has received to serve others, faithfully administering God's grace in its various forms." Sometimes it is not obvious how to apply our spiritual gifts, but if we truly look, there may be specific types of activities we could participate in that would fit our particular gifts.

How can utilizing your spiritual gifts help you deal with infertility?

_____

_____

_____

Having a baby or young children can certainly limit your participation at church. Many ministries are definitely easier without the complexity of childcare. If you do not already do so, you might consider volunteering to help or teach at your church. If you do not currently have any children, you may want to take the opportunity to go on a mission trip. If you have a strong desire to be around children, then you may enjoy helping in the nursery or assisting in youth programs, such as Sunday school classes, choir, or Vacation Bible School. In addition, you could offer your help at other local Christian ministry facilities. If God puts it in your heart to do something, you should pray about it and be willing to follow His direction.

Do you ever hesitate to get involved at your church? Why?

_____

_____

_____

Still Waiting

USE YOUR TIME

Many of us have dreams that for various reasons we do not accomplish. It could be that we have simply procrastinated, or it could be that we started then became too busy or disenchanted to finish. Sometimes it is because we have run into obstacles that may have prevented us from going farther, or because certain people have caused us to give up. Many times it seems that we abandon our goals and dreams because of practical responsibilities that seem to take precedence.

Do you have a dream (that does not involve motherhood) that you still have the desire to pursue?

_____

_____

_____

Sometimes we lack the skills or information needed to actualize our true goals. We may need to obtain more training or a higher degree. We may need to research other possibilities, different methods, procedures, or locations. We may need to give up something that we have in order to try something new. Sometimes, we may lack confidence or may have difficulty being willing to risk failure.

Is there anything that is holding you back from doing more?

_____

_____

_____

Having a baby almost automatically postpones other personal or professional plans. Even if you decide to return to work as soon as possible, other activities and involvements will inevitably take a backseat to raising your child. Usually free time becomes greatly diminished, if

Time and Service

not completely nonexistent. If God has delayed in giving you children at this time, then you should appreciate your free time and make the most of this opportunity to explore other areas of interest.

There are so many amazing things that we can do with our time. We can work, we can create and imagine, we can make things with our hands, and we can go see shows, exhibitions, or great works of art. We can learn a new hobby or attend a concert. If we have the resources and the inclination, we can travel all over the world or just get to know our own city. We can start our own business, or write, or organize, or communicate with family and friends. We can also help at a non-profit organization such as a school, a shelter, a museum, a symphony, a sports team, a cancer society, the Humane Society, etc. If you are willing, you can use your unique talents to make a real difference in the lives of people by simply donating your time and energy to do whatever is needed.

Do you feel that you truly value your time and use it effectively?

_____

_____

_____

Having a quiet time and praying are probably the most important ways we can spend our time. We can never pray too much or read God's word too often. When you pray for children, be persistent and remember Jeremiah 32:17, which reads:

> *Ah, Sovereign LORD, you have made the heavens and the earth by your great power and outstretched arm. Nothing is too hard for you.*

The Bible tells us in Colossians 3:23–24:

> Whatever you do, work at it with all your heart, as working for the Lord, not for men, since you know that you will receive an inheritance from the Lord as a reward. It is the Lord Christ you are serving.

Still Waiting

Even if our efforts do not seem outstanding or exemplary to others, we can be sure that God sees our hearts and knows everything we do, and He will reward us.

God deeply cares about you and has only the very best in mind for you. Let us strive with all our hearts to be like the person described in Jeremiah 17:7–8:

> *But blessed is the man who trusts in the LORD, whose confidence is in him. He will be like a tree planted by the water that sends out its roots by the stream. It does not fear when heat comes; its leaves are always green. It has no worries in a year of drought and never fails to bear fruit.*

Additional Resources

1. Stepping Stones
   http://www.bethany.org/step
   (616) 224 - 7488

2. Hannah's Prayer Ministries
   http://www.hannah.org
   (682) 365 - 4308

3. Sarah's Laughter
   http://www.sarahs-laughter.com
   (225) 926 - 2076

4. A Woman's Place
   http://www.waymarks.com/wmnplc/support.html

Facilitator's Guide

Overview

THIS STUDY WORKS well in eight sessions, with the first session as an introductory meeting and the last session as a final social event. As you meet together you will find that people seek out an infertility support group for many different reasons. Some couples may have only been trying for several months; some may have been trying for years; others may already be looking at adoption possibilities. Some of the participants will open up about their struggles, while others may never reveal the details of their situation. Be patient while the members of the group become comfortable with each other and begin to share their experiences. Also, remember that each group is different—feel free to skip a section that does not resonate with the individuals in your study. The purpose of this ministry is to provide encouragement, understanding, and hope.

The most important thing that you can do as a leader is to pray consistently for each person in the group. It is also a good idea to begin and end each session with prayer. The material in this study is positive and practical, and the suggested icebreaker questions below are neutral and not child related. However, be prepared for various responses. Have a box of tissues handy and be sensitive to individual needs. If someone becomes emotional, stop and have the group pray for that person. Your primary role is to foster friendship and support.

SESSION 1

The first meeting is a good opportunity to begin bonding the members of the group and to introduce the study. I recommend including the following:

1. Welcome everyone and open with prayer. Have them write down their contact information. Find out how many copies of the study you will need.
2. Take time to get to know each other briefly. Because the emotions tend to be right below the surface, try to avoid talking about pregnancy, children, etc. Below are a few suggestions for topics:

    Tell us about your family.
    Tell us about your job.
    Tell us about how you met your spouse.
    Do you usually go to church, and if so, where?

3. Go over the goals for the group, including the following:

    Sharing and support
    Encouragement and prayer
    Developing their relationship with God
    Developing as people
    Not about fertility treatments
    Importance of confidentiality

4. Share your own story. Also, explain the difference between primary and secondary infertility.
5. Explain how the study is organized in six weeks, divided into two parts. Mention that they should bring their Bibles with them. Remind them that completing this study does not mean that their struggle is eliminated.

Facilitator's Guide

6. Have a short devotion and remind them how special each of them are.

   Read 1 John 4:9–12 regarding God's love.
   Read Jeremiah 29:11 regarding God's plan for them.
   Read Galatians 6:2 and Psalm 68:19 regarding help for bearing burdens.

7. Repeat together, "I will trust God no matter what." Read Romans 15:13, and close with prayer.

SESSION 2

Begin each session with icebreaker questions to help everyone relax and get to know each other better. Below are a few suggestions:

   What is your favorite food?
   What is your favorite beverage?
   What is your favorite movie (either old or recent)?
   What is your middle name, and where did it come from?

The first chapter primarily involves reading scripture and making observations about the character of God. The content provides a foundation for the rest of the study. To prepare for this chapter, you may want to review the story of Abraham and Sarah (Gen. 12:1–7, 15:1–6, 16:1–6, 17:1–22, 18:1–15, 21:5 and Rom. 4:18–22).

SESSION 3

Below are a few suggestions for icebreaker questions:

   What is your favorite song (pop, church, etc.)?
   What was the best class you ever took in school?
   What is the best advice you have ever received?

The second chapter encourages participants to be honest about their feelings. Some of the questions are more personal, so make sure no one feels pressured to answer. Allow time after each question for the participants to think, and feel free to share your own thoughts, but I would recommend moving on if there does not seem to be anyone else wanting to contribute to the discussion. To prepare for this chapter, you may want to review the story of Isaac and Rebekah (Gen. 25:19–26), the story of Jacob, Leah, and Rachel (Gen. 29:31–35 and 30:1–24), the story of Hannah (1 Sam. 1:1–20), the parable of the sower (Mark 4:1–20), and the parable of the prodigal son (Luke 15:11–32).

SESSION 4

Below are a few suggestions for icebreaker questions:

Do you have any pets, and if so, what are they?
What was the most disastrous meal you've ever eaten or made?
What is the best birthday you ever had?

Many of the questions in the third chapter are very personal, so again, be sensitive if participants choose not to answer. For the third question in particular, "How have you kept the spark in your marriage," try to steer the discussion towards non-sexual, practical, everyday ideas, such as having a regular date night, writing notes to each other, and taking time off from trying to have a baby. To prepare for this chapter, you may want to review the story of Zechariah and Elizabeth (Luke 1:5–25).

At the beginning of either session four or five, begin discussing a social event for the last session. You may want to ask if one member of the group would be willing to organize the activity. That person will enjoy planning the event and will feel more involved in the group. The event could be a dinner together at a restaurant or an informal gathering at another location.

Facilitator's Guide

SESSION 5

Below are a few suggestions for icebreaker questions:

What was your first job?
What was the best place you have ever traveled?
What is your favorite Bible verse?

To prepare for this chapter, you may want to review the story of David (especially 1 Sam. 16:1–13 and 2 Sam. 5:1–5), and the parable of the persistent widow (Luke 18:1–8).

SESSION 6

Below are a few suggestions for icebreaker questions:

If you could receive one luxury service every day for a year, what would you choose?
What is one article of clothing (or one possession) of your spouse's that you would like to get rid of?
If you could invent a machine to do one task you dislike, what would you invent?

To prepare for this chapter, you may want to review Proverbs 31:10–31.

SESSION 7

Below are a few suggestions for icebreaker questions:

What is the best gift you ever received?
What is your favorite hobby?
If you could have any job in the world, what job would you choose?

Still Waiting

If you knew you could not fail, what is something (besides having a child) that you would like to do?

To prepare for this chapter, you may want to review the story of Deborah (Judg. 4:1–24), and the story of Priscilla and Aquila (Acts 18:1–4 and 18:18–28). You may also want to find a list of spiritual gifts with an explanation of each gift, in case members of the group have questions.

SESSION 8

Have fun and celebrate new friendships.

WinePressPublishing
Great Books, Defined.

To order additional copies of this book call:
1-877-421-READ (7323)
or please visit our website at
www.WinePressbooks.com

If you enjoyed this quality custom-published book,
drop by our website for more books and information.

www.winepresspublishing.com
"Your partner in custom publishing."

CPSIA information can be obtained at www.ICGtesting.com
Printed in the USA
LVOW060447151111

254953LV00001B/17/P